My Style

I love creating intricate black and white floral designs that start with focal points such as animals, faces, inspirational quotes, or mandalas. I always begin with a subject in mind, then add botanical details in the background. Some of my pieces are inspired by famous buildings around the world, and others are works of fantasy-inspired doodle art featuring forests, parks, waterfalls, etc. And I can't get enough of bold and bright colors on my drawings!

My Favorite Coloring Supplies

Here's a quick look at some of my preferred coloring media. But don't forget! You can also use crayons, water-based markers, gel pens . . . anything you like!

A. Fine-point felt-tip pens: Some of us love adding patterns on drawings while coloring; felt-tip pens are great for that. They are also good for adding colors inside small, detailed areas.

B. Colored pencils: For a smooth coloring experience, I highly recommend colored pencils. They are very easy to blend and great for layering colors.

C. Brush markers: These are your best choice if you want to achieve bright and vivid colors. Depending on the brand you use, they are very blendable. My favorites are Winsor & Newton and Copic Sketch markers.

D. Chisel-tip markers: These are good for coloring large areas. With the various angles of the tip, you can get three types of stroke: broad, medium, and thin. Colorless chisel-tip markers are also great to use as a blending tool.

E. Water-soluble pastels: If you want to add a splash of watercolor to your designs, use water-soluble pastels. They act like crayons when dry, but you have the option of applying water to add a watercolor wash to your work, and they are very easy to manipulate. You can even use an alcohol-based blender marker or a paper blending stump to blend the colors.

Coloring Tips

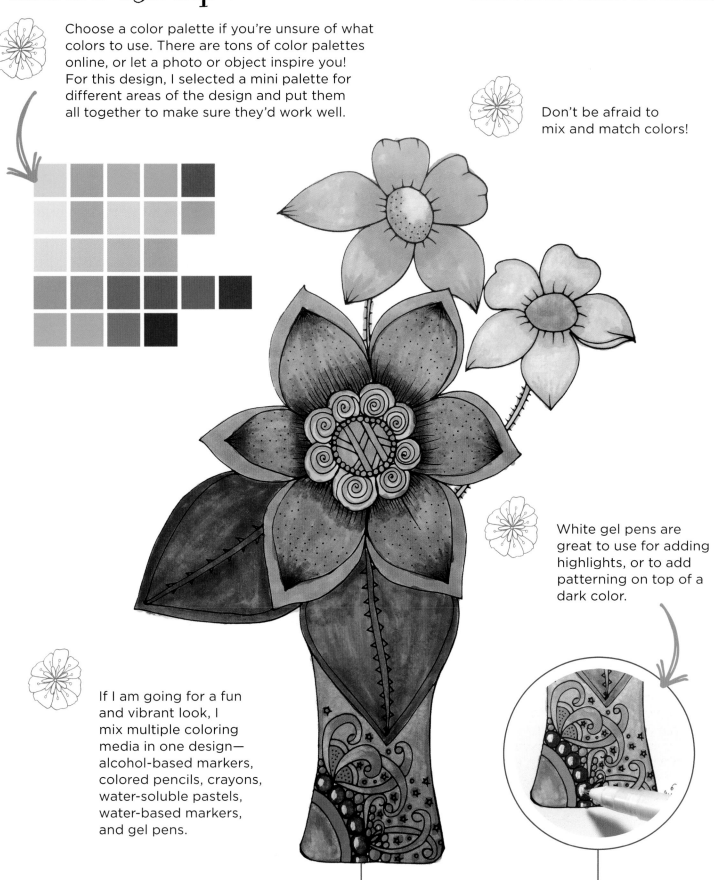

Choose a color palette if you're unsure of what colors to use. There are tons of color palettes online, or let a photo or object inspire you! For this design, I selected a mini palette for different areas of the design and put them all together to make sure they'd work well.

Don't be afraid to mix and match colors!

White gel pens are great to use for adding highlights, or to add patterning on top of a dark color.

If I am going for a fun and vibrant look, I mix multiple coloring media in one design— alcohol-based markers, colored pencils, crayons, water-soluble pastels, water-based markers, and gel pens.

How to Blend

I'm always going for the well-blended look. To achieve this, I use a good blender, though you can also blend without a blender by simply using several different shades of a single color and building up a gradient with them. But I like to use an **alcohol-based blender marker** with almost every coloring medium and design that I do. Blenders with chiseled tips are my favorite because they are versatile—you can get thick and thin lines and blends out of them. I usually begin with light pastel shades no matter what medium I'm using. That way I can slowly build the colors to bright, bold tones.

1. Fill the center of the flower with a light color, like this yellow.

2. Now use a darker color to go around the inner edges of the flower center, on top of the light color.

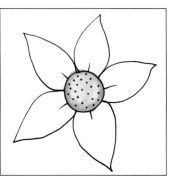

3. Blend the colors using a blending tool such as a blending marker, using gentle strokes and moving your tool from dark to light.

4. Fill in the petals with a new light color, like this orange.

5. Now use a darker color, like this dark orange, around the outer edges of the center of the flower.

6. This darker color at the base of the petals gives the flower dimensional, realistic "shadows."

7. Blend the colors using a blending tool such as a blending marker—chisel tips like this one are my favorite.

8. Your beautifully blended flower is done!

Coloring Leaves

When I color leafy drawings, I use many different shades of green. I also like to use two different color supplies: alcohol-based markers and colored pencils. Below, I'll walk you through my leaf process! Here are the two color palettes I used in this example.

Alcohol-based markers   *Colored pencils*

1. Pick the shades of green that you want to use.

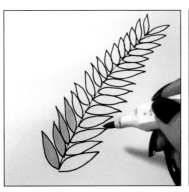

2. Start coloring with the lightest marker.

3. Pick a darker marker and begin coloring the corners of the leaves.

4. Fill in the outer corners of the leaves with the darker shade.

5. Start blending with an alcohol-based blender marker until the light and dark colors are nicely merged.

6. Color the stem or stem area with another darker green marker.

7. Use a colored pencil to add more depth to the leaves.

8. Begin tracing the outer edges of the leaves and stem with colored pencil.

9. Blend everything with the blender marker.

10. Now use a different, blue-green colored pencil around each leaf and stem.

11. Continue with the new color and blend until you're satisfied.

12. You're done!

Listening, page 45.

6 *Colored pencils (Prismacolor). Color by Kati Erney.*

Life Lessons, page 33.
Colored pencils (Faber-Castell, Prismacolor). Color by Lynette Parmenter.

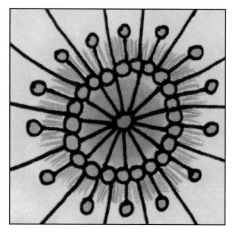

Neighbors, page 39.

Markers (Spectrum Noir), colored pencils (Faber-Castell), gel pens (Sakura), pastels. Color by Lisa Caryl.

Little Beauties, page 41.
Markers (Copic, Sharpie), colored pencils (Prismacolor), gel pen (Uni-Ball). Color by Keara Irby.

Welcome, page 35.

10 *Markers (Spectrum Noir), colored pencils (Prismacolor), gel pens (Sakura). Color by Lisa Caryl.*

Live and Let Live, page 37.
Markers (Copic, Prismacolor, Spectrum Noir), colored pencils (Prismacolor), soft pastels (Lyra). Color by Lisa Caryl.

Enchanted, page 65.

Colored pencils. Color by Lynette Parmenter.

Fab Fox, page 47.
Colored pencils (Marco Raffiné, Crayola), gel pens (Uni-Ball). Color by Keara Irby.   13

Strength, page 43.

Markers (Copic, Ironlak), colored pencils (Prismacolor), gel pens (Sakura). Color by Llara Pazdan.

Tree of Life, page 31.
Markers (Conda), colored pencils (Prismacolor). Color by Krisa Bousquet. 15

Forest Fellowship, page 17.

Colored pencils (Prismacolor, Crayola, Marco Raffiné), gel pen (Uni-Ball). Color by Keara Irby.

Those who dwell
among the beauties and mysteries of the earth
are never alone or weary of life.

—Rachel Carson

_____

_____

_____

_____

_____

_____

_____

_____

_____

Forest Fellowship

Listen to the voice of nature,
for it holds treasures for you.

—Native American proverb

A mountain with a wolf on it
stands a little bit higher.

—Russian proverb

_____
_____
_____
_____
_____
_____
_____
_____

Lone Wolf

Let's take our hearts
for a walk in the woods and listen
to the magic whispers of old trees.

—Unknown

_____

_____

_____

_____

_____

_____

_____

_____

_____

If you listen closely,
you can almost hear the earth breathe.

—Unknown

_____

_____

_____

_____

_____

_____

_____

_____

_____

_____

Sunshine Squirrel

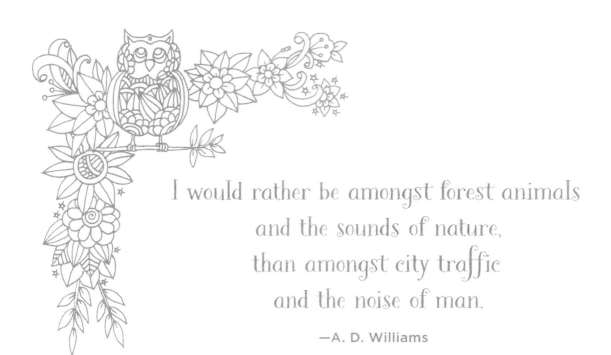

I would rather be amongst forest animals
and the sounds of nature,
than amongst city traffic
and the noise of man.

—A. D. Williams

Flower Fox

In the company of flowers
we know happiness.
In the company of trees
we are able to think.

—Unknown

I took a walk in the woods
and came out taller than the trees.

—Henry David Thoreau

Tree of Life

Pastel shades create a welcoming, gentle coloring
that fills you with contentment.

In every walk with nature
one receives far more than he seeks.

—John Muir

Life Lessons

A soft yellow background brings
an afternoon glow to this homey scene.

Plant dreams,
pull weeds,
and grow a happy life!

—Unknown

Welcome

Analogous yellow and green shades provide a
nice background for pops of color.

A true conservationist is a man
who knows that the world
is not given by his fathers,
but borrowed from his children.

—John James Audubon

Live and Let Live

Pastel shades of yellow and blue
give this finished piece a calming effect.

The environment
is where we all meet;
where all have a mutual interest;
it is the one thing all of us share.

—Lady Bird Johnson

_____

_____

_____

_____

_____

_____

_____

Neighbors

Create a soft feel with a blue gradient background like this one.

The poetry of earth is never dead.

—John Keats

_____

_____

_____

_____

_____

_____

_____

_____

_____

Little Beauties

Try sticking to just two complementary shades, like blue and orange, but use all different tints and shades of those colors.

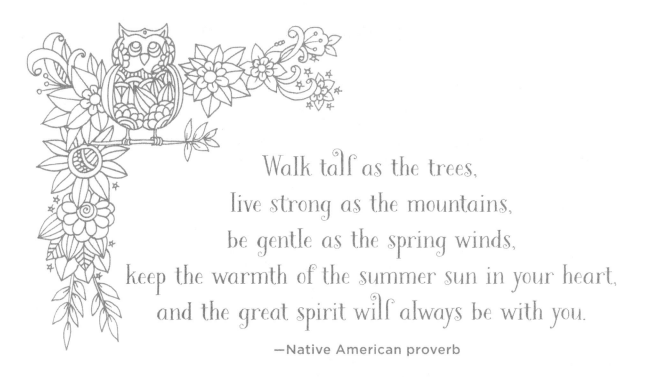

Walk tall as the trees,
live strong as the mountains,
be gentle as the spring winds,
keep the warmth of the summer sun in your heart,
and the great spirit will always be with you.

—Native American proverb

Strength

Don't forget that you can add new elements to a coloring design, like the clouds added here!

"Lots of people talk to animals,"
said Pooh.
"Not very many listen, though."

—Benjamin Hoff, *The Tao of Pooh*

_____
_____
_____
_____
_____
_____
_____
_____
_____
_____

Listening

Try using light pressure to achieve a gradient effect where
the background color radiates from the center and fades out into nothing.

Nothing is
more beautiful than
the loveliness of the woods before sunrise.

—George Washington Carver

Fab Fox

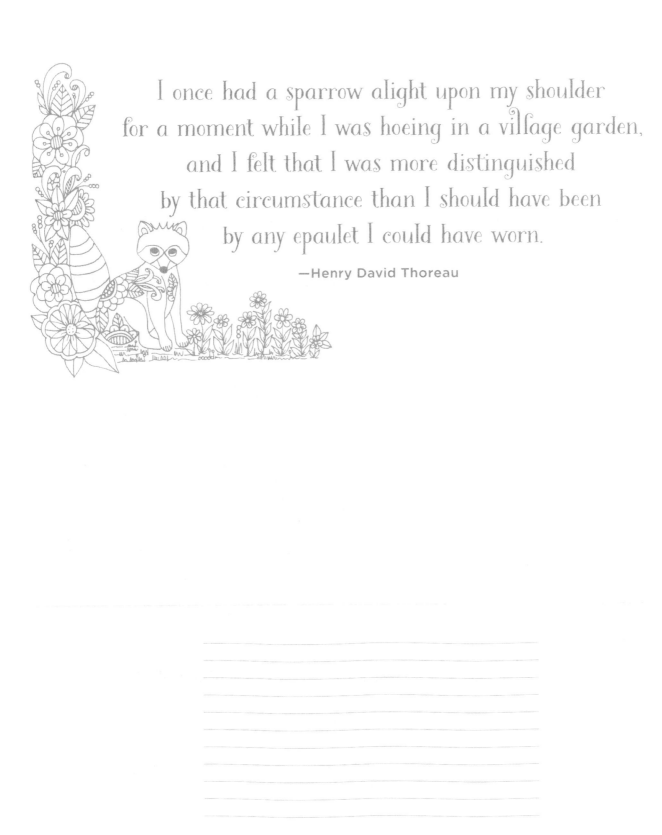

I once had a sparrow alight upon my shoulder
for a moment while I was hoeing in a village garden,
and I felt that I was more distinguished
by that circumstance than I should have been
by any epaulet I could have worn.

—Henry David Thoreau

A Little Birdie Told Me

Nature's peace
will flow into you
as sunshine flows into trees.

—John Muir

Flower Power

Come forth into the light of things,
Let Nature be your teacher.

—William Wordsworth, "The Tables Turned"

Professor

To sit in the shade
on a fine day, and look upon verdure,
is the most perfect refreshment.

—Jane Austen, *Mansfield Park*

The forest is for me a temple—
a cathedral of tree canopies
and dancing lights.

—Dr. Jane Goodall

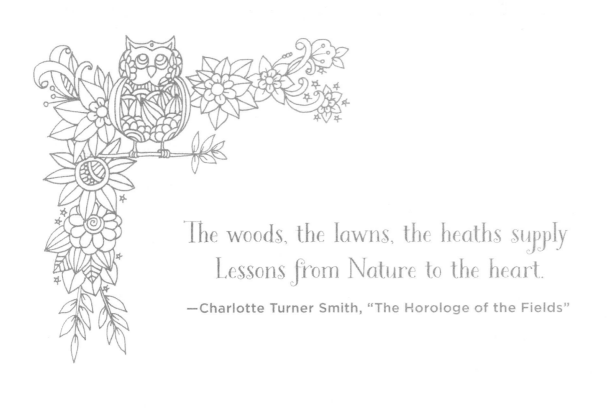

The woods, the lawns, the heaths supply
Lessons from Nature to the heart.

—Charlotte Turner Smith, "The Horologe of the Fields"

_____
_____
_____
_____
_____
_____
_____
_____

We are the earth,
made of the same stuff;
there is no other, no division between us
and "lower" or "higher" forms of being.

—Estella Lauter

The earth
has music for those who listen.

—George Santayana

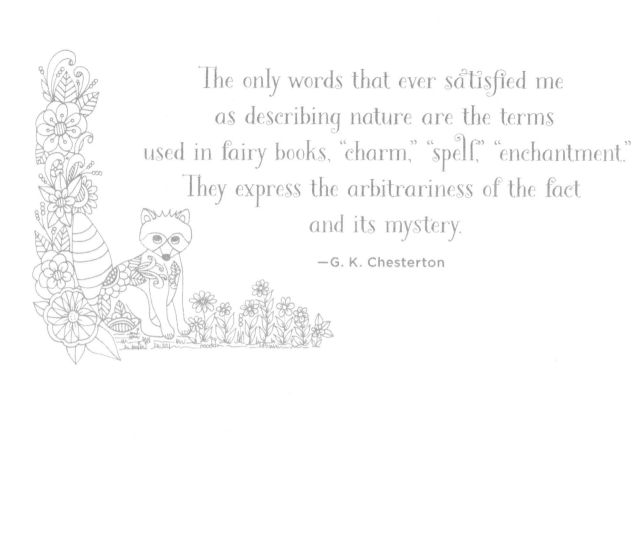

The only words that ever satisfied me
as describing nature are the terms
used in fairy books, "charm," "spell," "enchantment."
They express the arbitrariness of the fact
and its mystery.

—G. K. Chesterton

When a pine needle falls in the forest,
the eagle sees it,
the deer hears it,
and the bear smells it.

—Native American proverb

Observant Doe

69

Some old-fashioned things
like fresh air and sunshine
are hard to beat.

—Laura Ingalls Wilder

Vitality and beauty
are gifts of nature for those who live
according to its laws.

—Leonardo da Vinci

Deer

Forests are the lungs of our land,
purifying the air
and giving fresh strength to the people.

—Franklin D. Roosevelt

_____
_____
_____
_____
_____
_____
_____
_____
_____

Bunnies Bloom

Time spent among trees
is never wasted time.

—Katrina Mayer

_____
_____
_____
_____
_____
_____
_____
_____

Wilderness is not a luxury
but a necessity of the human spirit.

—Edward Abbey

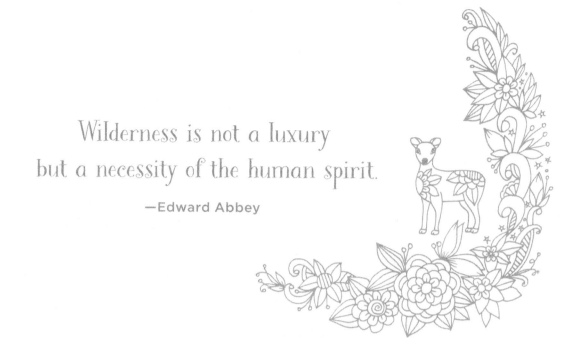

Rise and shine.
There is adventure waiting outside.

—Unknown

_____
_____
_____
_____
_____
_____
_____
_____